Th.

PA-KUA

PA-KUA

Chinese Boxing
for Fitness and Self-Defense

by Robert W. Smith

Kodansha International Ltd.

Distributed in the United States by Kodansha International/ USA Ltd., through Harper & Row, Publishers, Inc., 10 East 53rd Street, New York, New York 10022.

Published by Kodansha International Ltd., 12-21, Otowa 2-chome, Bunkyo-ku, Tokyo 112 and Kodansha International/USA Ltd., with offices at 10 East 53rd Street, New York, New York 10022 and The Hearst Building, 5 Third Street, Suite No. 430, San Francisco, California 94103. Copyright in Japan 1967 by Kodansha International Ltd. All rights reserved. Printed in Japan.

LCC 80-84589
ISBN 0-87011-462-X
ISBN 4-7700-0942-9 (in Japan)

First edition, 1967
First paperback edition, 1981
Third printing, 1983

Table of Contents

Acknowledgments

THE AUTHOR thanks the following persons for their assistance in the preparation of this work:

Editorial review: E. Gunberg and T. Stanhope
Functional review: B. Fusaro and D. Slater
Graphics: R. Mischke, W. Neisler, and R. Denny
Typewriting: S. Jackson

Others helped. The Davis Library in Bethesda, Md. provided serene surroundings and librarians whose eyes diplomatically dodged each time the author bounded from his chair to "walk through" a tactic. The author's wife proxied for him in building the patio and painting the house, further diminishing his prestige with his neighbors, but giving him time to write. The greatest debt, however, is owed Kuo Feng-ch'ih, his Pa-kua teacher in Taiwan. Paul (to use his Christian name) Kuo not only taught me the rudiments of the art but also posed for many of the photographs and reviewed the manuscript. To all who helped, the author says with H. Belloc:

> For no one, in our long decline,
> So dusty, spiteful and divided,
> Had quite such pleasant friends as mine,
> Or loved them half as much as I did.

In Place of an Introduction

THERE ARE few books even in Chinese on Pa-kua *Chang* (palm) or Pa-kua *Ch'uan* (boxing). This is not only the first book on the art in a foreign language, but also the first to present the circling method with its functions balanced against a more linear method which initially may have more appeal for Westerners. The more linear system is the result of three years of study under Huang I-hsiang (洪懿祥), senior student of Chang Chun-feng (張俊峯), one of the leading boxers in Formosa. For the classical circling method, I have used extensively the two best books written on the art to date, Sun Lu-t'ang's *Pa-kua Ch'uan Hsueh* ("*Study of Pa-kua Boxing*," Peking, 1916), and Huang Po-nien's *Lung Hsing Pa-kua Chang* ("*Dragon Shape Pa-kua Palm*," Shanghai, 1936). Master Sun, whose "eyes were very high" (meaning he stood above most boxers), is known and revered by many Chinese. His book forms the basis of the circling system presented here. Huang's book reveals how the art had been modified in the twenty years following issuance of the Sun text. To show the present circling methods, I have used the teaching of Kuo Feng-ch'ih (郭鳳墀), my personal teacher; Chen P'an-ling (陳泮嶺), the world's leading authority on Chinese boxing; and Wang Shu-chin (王樹金), pupil of famed Master Chang Chao-tung (張兆東).

Why write a book on a subject about which even few Chinese know? Simply, to inform Western readers about a discipline worthy of far wider recognition than it now has. Although Pa-kua is self-defense *par excellence*, it is also an excellent system of ex-

9

ercise which will enlarge one's physical, mental, and possibly even psychic horizons. *Physically*, it will tone and invigorate your muscles and sharpen and soothe your nerves, teaching you to relax and improving your overall health. *Mentally*, the bodily relaxation will produce a calm mind, one capable of great concentration. I leave it to someone more competent to enlarge on the psychic reward; suffice to say I believe there is one. Also, I have avoided using the word "character," but I insist that the practice of Pa-kua requires ever-increasing increments of self-discipline, and this cannot but have its impact. In the end Pa-kua will let you know and conquer yourself (like Mallory and his mountain, we only conquer ourselves). Only one with true self-knowledge can master others. This mastery comes, not from the muscles, but from the mind. But, paradoxically, seek to master others and it will elude you; seek to know yourself and you will achieve mastery. "If you ask how I strike the enemy, I cannot tell you: I only do my exercise," said Wan Lai-sheng about Master Tu Hsin-wu's natural boxing *Tzu Jan Men*, and the same holds for Pa-kua and the other internal methods, *t'ai-chi* and *hsing-i*.

Chinese books on Pa-kua boxing lay great stress on philosophical aspects which most Westerners would stamp as mysticism. My eschewing of most of these does not mean I disbelieve them. It merely means that I do not think a beginning text written for the Western reader is the place for philosophy—that too much philosophy would obfuscate material which by its very nature is difficult to present. Germanely, there is the delicious story of a philosopher in a boat asking the boatman if he knew philosophy. When the boatman replied in the negative, the philosopher sighed: "Ah, then you have lost half a life." A storm broke and the boat began to sink. The boatman asked the sage, "Do you know how to swim?" When the philosopher shook his head, the boatman said, "Ah, then you have lost all of a life!"

10

This book cannot teach you everything there is to know about Pa-kua. In the absence of a qualified teacher—I know of only a few in the U.S.—it can, however, serve as a substitute. Rose S. C. Li of the University of Michigan, who has spent a lifetime practicing Pa-kua and *tsing-i*, wrote me recently that "its delicate technique, theories, and philosophy are not easy for the Western mind to grasp." I more than half agree.

Therefore, this book is but an introduction and basic guide to a highly sophisticated exercise. It is brief because I didn't want to be like the man who said he knew how to spell *banana* but didn't know where to stop. Over two decades of learning and teaching non-Chinese fighting arts have provided some useful background for me. Pa-kua, however, is unlike and superior to the other arts I learned, and so, in 1959 when I began to practice it, I did so from scratch. I am still learning. Won't you join me?

I
Beginnings and Background

A. THE NAME AND THE PHILOSOPHY

Pa-kua (八卦), pronounced "ba-gwa," is one of the three branches of the *nei-chia* (internal family or system) of Chinese boxing—the other two are *t'ai-chi* and *hsing-i*. The name as well as the rationale derive from the system of philosophy growing out of the *I Ching (Book of Changes)*—3,000 years old, but timeless. Originally a manual of oracles, the *Book of Changes* evolved to ethical enumerations, eventually becoming a book of wisdom, one of the Five Classics of Confucianism. It became a common source for both Confucian and Taoist philosophy. The central theme of the book, as well as the system of boxing, is continuous change. While the book's basic idea, as Richard Wilhelm has said,* is the continuous change and transformation underlying all existence, the boxing absorbs this idea into a system of exercise and defense.

Originally the *Book of Changes* was a collection of linear signs to be used as oracles. In its most rudimentary sense these oracles confined themselves to the answers "yes" and "no." Thus a "yes" was written in a single unbroken line (————) and "no" in a single broken line (—— ——). Time brought a need for differentiation and amplification which required additional lines. Thus the eight tri-

---

* The Richard Wilhelm translation of the *Book of Changes*, with a foreword by C. G. Jung, will delight those desiring to read the work. It is in two volumes and published by Routledge & Kegan Paul Ltd. (reprinted in 1960). The *Book of Changes* has proved so fascinating for some that one European scholar learned Chinese (that disease and not a language) merely to read it. To the Chinese its study is not a thing to be taken lightly. Only those advanced in years regard themselves as ready to learn from it. Confucius himself is said to have been seventy years old when he first took up the *Book of Changes*.

grams (or lines of three ▬▬▬) evolved and, later, the eight hexagrams (or lines of six ▤▤▤). The Chinese word for both types of signs is *kua* (diagram). This, then, is the origin of the word *pa-kua*, or "eight diagrams."

The eight symbols that form the basis of the *Book of Changes* are as follows:

	Name	*Attribute*	*Image*
▬▬▬	Ch'ien, the Creative	Strong	Heaven
▬ ▬	K'un, the Receptive	Devoted, Yielding	Earth
▬▬_▬	Chen, the Arousing	Inciting Movement	Thunder
▬▬–▬	K'an, the Abysmal	Dangerous	Water
▬▬▬	Ken, Keeping Still	Resting	Mountain
▬▬▬	Sun, the Gentle	Penetrating	Wind, Wood
▬▬▬	Li, the Clinging	Light-giving	Fire
▬▬▬	Tui, the Joyous	Joyful	Lake

In turn these trigrams are formed into a diagram representing the Primal Arrangement (Sequence of Earlier Heaven) inside and the Inner-World Arrangement (Sequence of Later Heaven) outside. The seasons as well as cardinal directions (note that the Chinese place south at the top) are embraced by these phenomena *(see Fig. 1)*.

You need not comprehend the *Book of Changes* to practice the boxing, but the basics presented above are helpful in understanding the evolution and origin of the boxing system. In a word, Pa-kua boxing* is concerned with change; all is flux, nothing stands still. Technically, this rationale of change is its strength and its totality.

---

* Hereafter the word Pa-kua refers to the boxing method rather than the philosophy.

14

Fig. 1 Pa-kua diagram

B. ORIGIN AND GREAT MASTERS

No one knows the origin of Pa-kua. It is only known that Tung Hai-ch'uan (董海川) of Wenan Hsien in Hopeh Province during the Ch'ing Dynasty (A.D. 1798–1879) learned this art from an anonymous Taoist in the mountain fastnesses of Kiangsu Province. Tung, a young man then barely into his twenties, is said to have been nearly dead of starvation when the hermit chanced upon him. The Taoist ministered to him and Tung stayed several years with him and from him learned a "divine" boxing.

After becoming famous in Peking, Tung was challenged by Kuo Yun-shen (郭雲深) ("Divine Crushing Hand") of the *Hsing-i* school. Through two days of the duel, Kuo (who had killed men with his famous crushing hand) could not gain any advantage. On the third

15

day Tung took the offensive and so completely defeated Kuo that he made him a lifelong friend. Thereupon they signed a brotherhood pact requiring *hsing-i* students to take Pa-kua training and vice versa. For this reason—a most unusual denouement by anyone's standards—the systems are to this day coupled and complementary.

Near middle age, Tung became a eunuch in the king's palace. He did not get on with his fellows, however, and soon was assigned to the royal family of Su Ch'in-wang as a servant. Su employed a Mohammedan boxer and his wife as chief protectors of the household. Sha Hui-tzu, the boxer, held everyone to immediate obedience, and his wife, an expert pistol shot, made them a solid combination. Once at a big banquet where the congestion was beyond relief, Tung served tea to the guests by lightly scaling the wall and crossing the roof to the kitchen and back. Lord Su recognized from this that Tung probably had boxing ability. Subsequently, he ordered Tung to show his art. Tung did: he demonstrated Pa-kua. His sudden turns and fluid style enthralled the audience. Thereupon, Sha challenged Tung but was defeated. Tung watched for Sha to attempt revenge. Late one night Sha crept into Tung's bedroom, a knife in hand, while his wife aimed her pistol through the window at Tung. Tung quickly took the pistol from her and turned on Sha, who pounded his head on the floor seeking forgiveness. Tung agreed to forgive him and even accepted Sha as a student.

Later in life Tung retired and taught only a few selected persons his Pa-kua. Although he withered, the stories did not.* One had him in the midst of several men with weapons who were bent on his blood. He not only emerged unscathed, but soundly beat his attackers. Another time he sat in a chair leaning against a wall. The

---

* Lest the reader scoff too resoundingly, let him heed the words of R. H. Tawney: "Legends are apt, however, to be as right in substance as they are wrong in detail."

16

Fig. 2   Master Yin Fu

wall collapsed and his disciples ran up, fearful that he had been
buried. He was found nearby sitting in the same chair leaning
against another wall! But the grandest story, told by Wan Lai-
sheng, concerns Tung's death. Certain that he was dead, some of
his students attempted to raise the casket prior to burial. But the
casket would not move. It was as though it were riveted to the
ground. As his students tried again and again to lift it, a voice came
from inside the casket: "As I told you many times, none of you
has one-tenth my skill!" He then died and the casket was moved
easily.

Tung died at eighty-four. His most famous students (of a re-
ported total of only seventy-two) were: Yin Fu (尹復), Ch'eng
T'ing-hua (程廷華), Ma Wei-chi (馬維祺), Liu Feng-ch'un (劉鳳春),
and Shih Liu (史六).

Yin Fu (nicknamed "Thin Yin") was a native of I-hsien in Hopeh
Province *(see Fig. 2)*. Although his skill was superior he taught

17

Fig. 3   Master Li Ts'un-i   Fig. 4   Master Sun Lu-T'ang

few students. For his livelihood he guarded the residence of a nobleman. He died in 1909 at the age of sixty-nine. Some sources claim that he was a pupil of Ch'eng T'ing-hua rather than of Tung.

Ch'eng T'ing-hua, also a native of Hopeh, was nicknamed "Invincible Cobra Ch'eng." Besides teaching Pa-kua he ran a spectacles shop in Peking.* One story has it that during the Allied occupation of Peking in the Boxer Rebellion the foreigners were looting, raping, and killing. Ch'eng is said to have rushed from his house with a knife concealed under each armpit and to have killed at least a dozen Germans before being shot to death. Others claim the story is apocryphal and that Ch'eng died a natural death.

---

* Whence derived his nickname *Cobra*. Europeans especially refer to the cobra as the "eyeglass snake" (in German, *brillenschlange*).

18

Ch'eng's students included Li Ts'un-i (李存義) *(see Fig. 3)*, Sun Lu-t'ang (孫禄堂) *(see Fig. 4)*, Chang Yu-kuei (張玉魁), Han Ch'i-ying (韓奇英), Feng Chun-i (馮俊義), K'an Ling-feng (闞齡峯), Chou Hsiang (周祥), Li Han-chang (李漢章), Li Wen-piao (李文彪), and Ch'in Ch'eng (秦成).

Ma Wei-ch'i taught Sung Yung-hsiang (宋永祥), Sung Ch'ang-jung (宋長榮), Liu Feng-ch'un (劉鳳春), Liang Chen-p'u (梁振普), Chiang Chan-kuei (張占魁), Chih Lu (史六), and Wang Li-te (王立德). Some sources believe Ma was taught by Ch'eng T'ing-hua rather than by Tung himself.

The line has proliferated much since then. Greats nearer our own time are Shang Yun-hsiang (尚雲祥), Li Wen-pao (李文豹), Keng Chi-shan (耿繼善), and Chang Chao-tung (張照東). Chang Chao-tung *(see Fig. 5)*, a native of Hopeh Province, was expert in both Pa-kua and *hsing-i*. Each year Chang returned to his home in Ho-chien Hsien from Tientsin to visit his parents. The year he

Fig. 5   Master Chang Chaa-Tung

was sixty he returned to find a forty-year-old named Ma installed as the leading boxer. Ma approached Chang and politely told him that he could withstand his punch. (This was the usual way of deciding who was the strongest boxer—each would get a free swing at the other's body. The loser, however, had the option of challenging for an actual contest if he was unsatisfied with the one-punch method.) Chang obliged smilingly but ordered four students to hold a blanket in back of Ma. He then told Ma: "Put your hands up to protect your body. I will only hit your arm." So saying, Chang hit Ma's arm with his fingers and palm-butt. Ma immediately fell back sharply into the blanket, pulling all four students atop him. Ma knelt down and became a student of Chang.

The best-known Pa-kua boxers in Taiwan today are Wang Shu-chin (王樹金), Chang Chun-feng (張俊峯), Ch'en P'an-ling (陳泮嶺), Kuo Feng-ch'ih (郭鳳墀), and Hung I-hsiang (洪懿祥).

II
A Beginning Method

To APPRECIATE the classical circling method of Pa-kua, which will be described later, we begin with a description of a method easier to understand and assimilate and yet one which does not defile the overall *idea* of the art. This is a method taught by Chang Chun-feng in Taiwan. Chang claims to have learned Pa-kua under Chang Chao-tung, but this method contains so little of that master's classic style that it must be supposed that he learned it from some other teacher in the Tientsin area. I practiced with Chang for three hours one rainy afternoon in Taipei in 1960—a short time but long enough to see and feel his considerable skill. Illness prevented his teaching me on a regular basis, but I was able to learn his method from two of his senior students, Hung Hsien-mien and Hung I-hsiang. Before I left Taiwan I had learned the basic sixty-four postures and enough auxiliary movements to bring the total to over one hundred. I was not able, however, to photograph the system and have had to rely on my notes. Here we can only sample the whole, selecting postures that best illustrate the general principles.

A. THE EIGHTEEN EXERCISES
Each of the exercises that follow conform to the principles of Pa-kua, even though some have crept in from *hsing-i* and other systems. Practice them well, and, when you meet them in the postures, you can incorporate them with facility. Moreover, with these ex-

ercises learned, you will be able to create your own actions. And it is well to dwell on this a moment: a tactic is only that, a tactic. Principles are far more important, for with these we can invent, change, and refine other tactics.

First off, let's look at the principles underlying this type of Pakua.

    (1) Because the palm is more powerful and flexible than the fist, it is the major weapon used in Pa-kua.

    (2) The opponent must be stretched or unbalanced if an attack is to have the desired effect.

    (3) Your arms move only as part of your body.

    (4) Every action is circular; this imparts speed and power.

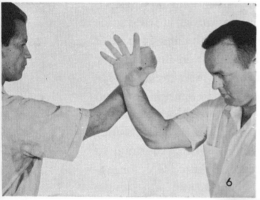

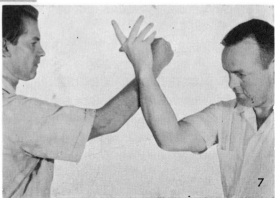

(5) To attack a strong antagonist you must *cross* either his body or his arm, preferably both. That is, do not attack directly, but rather obliquely by "turning his corner" and then attacking. To *cross* his arm(s) means that, as he attacks, you deflect and in the same movement seize his arm *(see Figs. 6–9)*.

(6) In pushing, hold your hands together and push slightly upward, thus destroying your opponent's root and propelling him backward.

(7) The waist is along the major axis of the body. Let it lead every action.

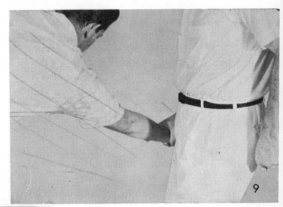

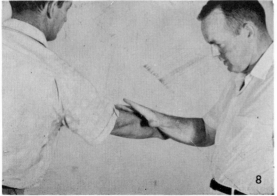

23

1. THE HAND SWORD *(Figs. 10–17)*

With your left fist at your left side, extend your right arm, with the hand opened and the palm up. The fingers of your right hand are held together and your arm, though extended, is not stretched, lest it afford a locking opportunity for your opponent. Keep your shoulder down throughout. Slowly turn your waist in a movement that turns the right arm in a chopping motion from right to left. Keep your knees bent slightly, and let your eyes follow the attack-

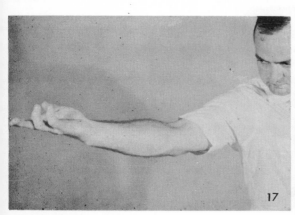

ing hand. When your arm and upper torso cannot turn farther left-ward, turn your right palm down and return to the right. Then do the same movement with your left hand. Now notice the close-up in Fig. 17: the shoulder is down, the elbow slightly bent. After several weeks of practice, spread your legs farther apart and do the action. The essence of this exercise is to mesh the actions of waist and arm.

2. DIRECT CLAMPING *(Figs. 18–23)*

Take a wide stance with your fists at your sides. Put your right hand in front of your left leg and, with the elbow bent, turn your waist and arm down to the left to a point beyond your left leg *(Fig. 19)*. Now turn waist and arm to the right, shifting your weight more to your right foot. When your arm goes past your right leg, turn it in a big counterclockwise circle as your body rises *(Fig. 21)*. Continue turning it and your waist to the left until you return in front of your left leg *(Fig. 23)*. Follow the movement of the hand with your eyes. Repeat with your left hand by simply reversing directions. Remember: your bent arm turns and moves only in conjunction with your waist.

3. REVERSE CLAMPING *(Figs. 24–28)*

This exercise merely reverses *Direct Clamping*. Beginning at your right leg, roll to the left with your waist and bent right arm. When you reach your left leg, turn your arm in a clockwise circle, rise, and return to the right. Your eyes follow the movement. Repeat with your left hand. The discerning student will see three circles in these actions: (1) the waist moving directly right or left, (2) the torso falling and rising, and (3) the overturning of the attacking hand. The target for this clamp is just under your opponent's nose.

4. DEFLECTION ATTACK *(Figs. 29–37)*

With your fingers open, bring your right hand, palm down, to eye level. Hold the palm cupped. This simulates a block. Now, without extending or altering the position of your arm, push to the left and down, the body leading the arm. As your arm nears your left knee, flatten your right palm. A fuller variation of this action is seen in Figs. 33–34. Here, as your left hand protects your groin, you turn to the right and your right hand comes to forehead level. Now,

turn your waist to the left as you pump down. In the function *(Figs. 35–37)* you may see it more clearly. Your opponent strikes with his left hand, which you deflect. From here you may pump down immediately or await his response. If he pushes down on your right hand then, of course, he provides impetus for your pumping action. If he throws his right hand—the Chinese believe that this "empties" the left side, making it vulnerable—you merely pump down as he strikes with his right fist, raising your left for protection.

5. Double-Duty Palm *(Figs. 38–46)*

Keeping your shoulder down, turn your waist to the left and chop down until your bent right arm passes your left leg. Returning to the right, bow your wrist and use the ridge as an attacking member. This simulates a downward chop at an opponent's throat, recovery, and a wrist-ridge attack to his midsection. For details see the photos, but, again, the key is to let your arm move only as a part of your body, never independently. A slightly different application is seen in Figs. 44–46. Here, as you withdraw your right leg, you chop inward (at opponent's attacking arm) and then, stretching your leg, you attack over his arm with your wrist-ridge.

33

47

48

34

6. CIRCLING AND REVERSE PUSH *(Figs. 47–50)*

Turn your waist to the left and circle your bent right arm as far as it will go. Then, pivoting on your elbow, push your right palm obliquely downward to the right as your body stretches on a line.

49

50

35

7. SQUATTING ATTACK *(Figs. 51–55)*

This exercise is truly functional in that it provides *vertical* leverage where no *horizontal* leverage is possible. Suppose you are caught in a tiny room with no area of lateral movement open to you. In such an instance, whether attacked from front or rear, you simply squat and use a hand-thrust attack. By lowering your body into a squat and at the same time thrusting out left and down, you create impact. Rising, clench your right hand in a fist at your side. Then, squatting again, use your right palm-butt obliquely leftward and rear *(Fig. 55 is a rear shot of this action)*. Rising, use your left hand, merely reversing the instructions for the right hand. Your target in these actions would be the opponent's groin or midriff.

36

37

8. Cross and Push *(Figs. 56–59)*

This exercise must be mastered if the postures are to be done correctly, for it enters into most of them. First take the straight-ahead posture (which actually is the *hsing-i* basic posture), with your left foot ahead. Your left arm is slightly bent and your eyes focus on the fingertips. Your right hand is open protecting the groin. Forty percent of your weight is on the front foot and 60 percent on the back foot, which is turned 60° outward *(Fig. 56)*. **(Hereafter this is called the 4–6 posture.)** Now as you pull your left hand back to

your left side, thrust your right arm obliquely to the left *(Fig. 57)*.
Pulling your right hand back toward your right side, take a short
step forward with your left foot, turn to the right and crouch as in
Fig. 58, both fists at your sides. Finally *(Fig. 59)*, take your right
foot forward, put it down so that it is perpendicular knee-to-toes,
stretch your body, and push upward, both hands held close together
(you may interlock the thumbs). Your left leg is nearly straightened
by the expansiveness of the move. Alternate sides after mastering
the initial action.

9. SPEAR HAND *(Figs. 60–66)*

Take a deep stance. Extend your left arm with the palm up. Now, turn your left hand over, clench your fingers, and begin to pull back to your left side. Simultaneously, spear out with your right hand, palm up *(Figs. 60–62)*. Then, turning your right hand over, pull back and let the left spear come out *from under* the withdrawing hand (not illustrated). The hand going out and the hand coming in must move as one. The function of this exercise is that you cross

the opponent's arm, pull him into you and, at the same time, spear him with the opposite hand. An elaboration of this tactic is seen in Figs. 63–66. Here, after spearing, circle your right hand counter-clockwise with your body and then thrust it forward again. Imagine catching an opponent's left triceps from underneath. Your counterclockwise circle pulls him forward, and then you quickly release him and spear his armpit.

10. PECKING *(Figs. 67–72)*

As you block by bringing your right arm up to eye level, put your fingers together and then peck forward, your arm moving in concert with your upper torso. This is a specialized striking technique. Your fingers together can attack the opponent's throat or, apart, his temple. See the use illustrated in Figs. 70–72.

11. Fist-Knuckle Double Impact Punch *(Figs. 73–76)*

From a wide stance, practice striking directly forward with a standing fist* from under your nose. The bottom part of the fist strikes first, and then the protruding knuckle of the index finger is brought down in a second impact. Use both hands. In looking at the photos,

---

* A standing fist is simply a fist held vertically rather than horizontally (flat).

pay attention to the body as the fist goes outward. The fist, remember, is merely an extension of the body. Above all, keep your shoulder down to enhance the power of the strike and to avoid opening up your armpit to his counter.

12. CORKSCREW PUNCH *(Figs. 77–82)*

From the basic 4–6 posture, take your right foot forward and place only the toes down as you deflect downward with your right arm, the palm up. Next, as your right foot spins and the heel falls, turn your fist counterclockwise and punch forward and down. Alter-

natively, you may deflect with your right arm as your left foot toes out, then follow through. This is shown in Figs. 80–82. Note here that the deflection is elbow followed by the knuckles of your right hand.

13. BIG CHOPPING *(Figs. 83–87)*

From the basic 4–6 posture, swing forward with a big right step as your left hand pulls back toward your left side and your entire right arm travels in a big arc forward and counterclockwise. In the function shown in Figs. 86–87, for variety, we use the left side. Your opponent throws a right hand. You *cross* with your right, grasp his wrist and pull him forward as your right leg goes forward and your left arm chops at the base of his skull. This is a short response necessitated by his attack when your left foot is forward. Had your right foot been forward, you would have derived much more power by taking your left foot forward with the left arm chop. As it is, you can still get added impetus by advancing your left foot and putting it down on or near his right foot.

85

86

87

49

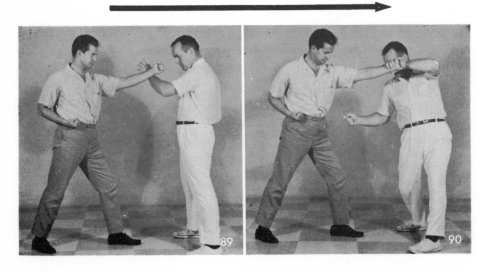

14. KNUCKLE PUNCH *(Figs. 88–92)*

This technique is my modification of the basic horse-riding posture punch of Chinese boxing. Practice deflecting with your left arm while stepping forward with your right foot and following with your left foot. Still retaining your hold with your left hand, strike with a standing fist against his side. If you have moved correctly, your opponent's feet and your own should be on a straight line *(see Fig. 88)*. I developed the method shown here as a quicker response, but, as I do it, I *image* the horse posture even though my feet do not move. Look at the photos. Your opponent tries a left hand which you *cross* and grasp. Retaining your hold, swing your torso through, and, using your right index knuckle, strike his left external obliques. Make a circle of it and you will master it. Only a slight touch at this soft point will suffice to show its vulnerability.

COPPERFIELD'S BOOKS

140 Kentucky St. Petaluma, Ca 762-0563
new and used books
must be returned with receipt
within 30 days for cash or credit.
Without receipt exchange only.

8718 Reg 3 8:02 pm 10/12/99

S USED BOOKS   1 @   6.50   6.50
S X14
SUBTOTAL   6.50
SALES TAX - 7.5%   .49
TOTAL   6.99
CASH PAYMENT   7.00
CHANGE   .01

peace on earth

15. FOLDING ELBOW *(Figs. 93–95)*

As you employ a standing fist, your opponent knife-blocks it outward to his right. Relaxing your entire arm, fold it at the elbow, take a half-step forward with your right foot, and elbow his middle. The actions shown as functions must be practiced 100 times solo for every time with a partner.

16. Scooping Foot *(Figs. 96–98)*

Pa-kua makes little use of the feet in attacking, but this one is useful. The same technique may be seen in Shao-lin boxing. As you scoop his advanced (or preferably, advancing) right foot, you may add pressure with your hands (not shown). What is depicted is a feint at scooping. You fake a scoop, your opponent raises his leg and, thinking he has escaped, puts it down. But, as he raises his foot, you retract your scoop foot circularly, and as he puts his foot down you snap it edgewise at his kneecap. Judoists knowing *ko-uchi-gari* will find this easy.

96

17. UPPERCUT *(Figs. 99–106)*

Practice stepping forward with your right foot as you loop your right arm (double impact: elbow-knuckles) forward in a deflection. Lower your body slightly as you deflect, then immediately rise, driving your right fist (palm up) into your opponent's heart. Again and always, the circle. Functionally, if in stepping forward you step on his foot, this will add pain and will prevent his taking the foot rearward. The uppercut is obscured in Fig. 103, but the body is there and that is the important thing. Let the body do the work. This principle is not alien to Western boxing. Rocky Marciano in training his uppercut always aimed for his own chin and let his body lead the punch, instead of uppercutting off a bag or ball. You can test the power of this rising strength by using your partner's shoulder. First slap downward with the back of your hand, clench your fist and shift your weight forward and slightly upward as your right fist uppercuts *(see Figs. 104–106)*.

56

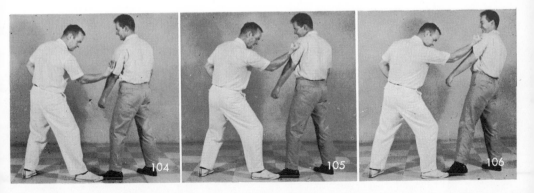

107

18. DEFLECTION AND REVERSE STRIKE *(Figs. 107–110)*

By now you should be able to look at the function and establish the solo exercise. With your feet on a line and your knees bent, do exactly what is shown in the function photos (i.e., photos that show the technique as used against an opponent), but without moving your feet. All you need to remember is (1) circle and (2) use your body, not your arms. The right hand is obscured in the final picture: it has turned over, the elbow is up, fingers down and open, and it strikes your opponent just below his navel.

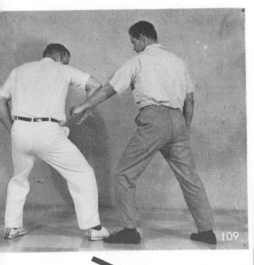

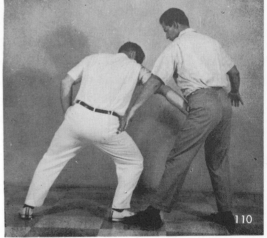

59

B. THE FORMS AND FUNCTIONS

We turn now to twenty basic forms. Some of the bloom is already off the rose in that the *Exercises* are the basis of the *Forms*. But the *Forms* themselves give rigor and system to Pa-kua and are easier to remember than the many attack and defense fragments seen in the *Exercises*. Do the *Forms* on both sides for all-around balance.

1. To Open (K'ai) *(Figs. 111–129)*

FORM: From the basic 4–6 posture, bring your left hand, palm down, directly ahead and parallel with your navel. At the same

60

time toe-out with your left foot (which means you are going up over this foot) *(Fig. 112)*. As you bring your right foot forward and put only the toes down a fist-width in front of your left foot, swing your right arm clockwise from down to up in a circle *(Figs. 113–14)*. Simultaneously, your left hand turns slightly counterclockwise near your right elbow. Carrying both hands in a full circle, lower your body slightly and push off your left foot as your right palm strikes forward and your left hand is held at your right elbow for defense *(Figs. 115–16)*. Notice that the right knee is on a line with the toes and that there is a straight line from your scalp to your left sole *(Fig. 117)*. You may hold this expanded posture or

you may, after stretching, bring your left foot forward half the distance to your right foot. In order to link with another action, however, you must follow-step.

FUNCTION: As your opponent strikes with his right fist, depress it with your left palm *(Fig. 118)*. If he resists by pushing upward, immediately step forward with your right foot as your right arm circles clockwise, rolling around his arm and grasping his forearm as your left grasps his elbow *(Fig. 119)*. Pull him forward and down toward your right side *(Figs. 120–21)*. As he resists by pulling back, strike him with your right palm as your body extends with your right foot forward *(Figs. 122–23)*. Curiously, the stronger the opponent, the easier it is to roll his arm. If, as you depress his arm, he relaxes it, be wary; you may be arguing with the wrong man. An alternative use is shown in Figs. 124–126.

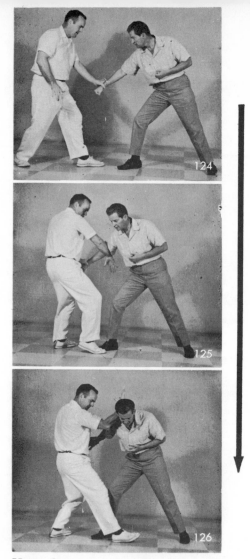

Here, for speed the right arm strikes the elbow and is whipped circularly up to his head. Your body moves as in the basic action. Although this is speedier than the arm-roll, it is not as sure, because you do not have the control, and his posture is not as broken. If, when he feels you depress his right hand, he crosses with his left hand, simply turn it in with your right shoulder and

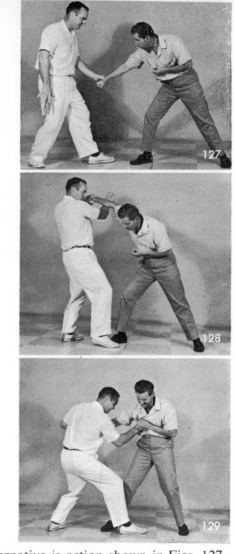

continue the action. An alternative is action shown in Figs. 127–29. Here, you attempt to roll his arm but he pushes downward, preventing your turning it. Simply take his downward resistance as impetus and thrust your right hand forward to his chest as your right leg goes forward. This action is straight ahead and does not involve *crossing* his body.

2. To Hold Up (P'eng) *(Figs. 130–137)*

FORM: As you pull your left hand to your left side, your right foot goes obliquely forward to the right. Then your left foot goes forward a fist-width in front of your right foot, only the toes touching. Simultaneously, both your hands are held near your left side. Now push off your right foot by carrying your left foot forward until your right leg is stretched straight, and push with both palms toward your left oblique.

FUNCTION: The direction of the *Form* tells you that you have turned your opponent's corner. Cross his body but first cross his arm. As he strikes with his left fist, cross from outside with your left (for

leverage on its return, first turn your left arm counterclockwise as far as it will go). As you pull his arm back toward your left side, step obliquely forward near his left foot with your right foot (to go beyond his left foot is even better, though much more difficult to accomplish). Then, bring your left foot on its toes in front of your right foot and, pushing off the right foot, take your left foot forward as both your hands push his left external obliques. A valuable aspect of the Pa-kua regimen is that in practice you push, whereas in a real fight the unbalancing push is transformed into a strike. This *Form* is extremely important. Practice it many times, going both left and right.

67

3. To Shake (Tun) *(Figs. 138–145)*

FORM: With your left foot, step obliquely left until your right leg is straight. Simultaneously, spear obliquely right with your right arm, palm up and screwed, while your left hand protects your groin and your left foot toes out. Now, take your right foot on its toes in front of your left as your left arm goes up, palm up, to where your right arm rests on the inner bend of your left elbow. Puil both hands down and outside of your right foot and, pushing off your left foot, push right obliquely with both hands.

FUNCTION: Your opponent tries a left. Block from inside with your right as your left foot goes obliquely forward to the left. As your right foot comes forward on its toes, swing your left arm upward to lock-strike his left elbow. Turning your hands over and grasping his arm, pull him toward your right foot. Then, step forward with your right foot and push him with both hands.

4. TO FEEL (T'AN) *(Figs. 146–156)*

FORM: As you toe-out with your left foot, pull your left hand back to your left side in a fist and underspear with your right palm obliquely left. Next, bring your right hand back to your right side in a fist as your right foot goes forward on its toes and the two leading fingers on your left hand thrust forward. Then, as your right foot goes forward, your right palm-butt pounds forward as your left hand returns to your left side.

FUNCTION: Your opponent tries a left-hand strike. You cross from outside with your left and pull him toward your left side. At the same time, spear along his arm with your right hand, palm up, to his throat. Because you still have his left hand, he reacts in the only way possible—by raising his right hand to deflect your right thrust upward. Thus he makes a cross of the two arms, and you thereupon

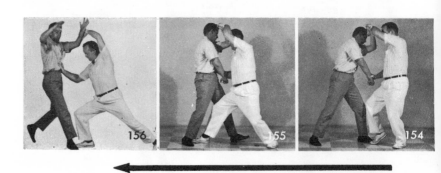

147   146

pull his right arm toward your right side while releasing your hold
on his left wrist. As he is pulled in, you meet him by putting your
right toes down in front of your left and by holding two fingers by
your chin. The pull brings his eyes athwart the fingers. If he raises
his left arm to fend off your two-finger attack, release your hold on
his right hand and take your right hand and foot forward in the
final attack. In this technique you stay one jump ahead of the
defender. If he reacts to one attack, he sets himself up for another.
Be careful of the eye attack, however: in practice do it alone, or if
with a colleague, have him turn his head (he will need no urging;
again look at the picture). A reminder: photos and description
leave out one decisive factor—simultaneity—as your left hand pulls
back, your right hand goes out. It must occur all at once or the
technique may fail.

153   152   151   150

161   160

5. To Erect (Li) *(Figs. 157–165)*

FORM: As you take your left foot to the left oblique, your left hand circles counterclockwise. Now take your right foot ahead of your left and rest it on its toes while your right arm also circles high. Both hands end the circle outside your right foot. Push off your left foot with both hands to the right oblique.

FUNCTION: Your opponent strikes with his right hand, which you block from inside with your circling left. Continuing your toe-out with your left foot, take your right foot forward on its toes and lock-strike his right elbow with your high-circling right. Both of your hands then grasp his right forearm and pull him toward your right foot. As he resists by rising, step obliquely forward with your right foot and push his midriff with both hands. In the photos the attacker has his right foot back, which prevents a full *cross* on his body. The technique works better when his right foot is advanced. Even in the example shown, however, his posture is broken sufficiently for you to attack decisively.

72

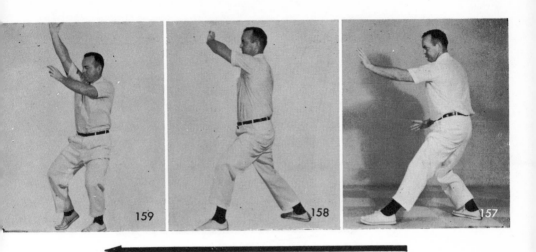

6. To Rebut (T'iao) *(Figs. 166–174)*

FORM: Depress with your left hand as you toe-out with your left foot. As your right foot comes on its toes ahead of your left, carry your right hand clockwise, wedging high. Next, loop your left fist in a counterclockwise circle and hammer forward with it as your right foot drives forward. Lean forward slightly with your body as you hammer; it is the body, not the arm, which has the power. Following this movement, your right hand circles clockwise and hammers forward with your body as your right foot takes another step forward.

FUNCTION: This may be done with equal effect against either hand. Your opponent tries a right and you depress with your left. He pulls his right arm up and immediately you step forward and lock-strike his elbow from underneath. (Do not hit his forearm lest he fold on you and stick his elbow in your ribs!) Releasing his right wrist, hammer toward the base of his skull with your left fist. To offset this, he will shift his right arm upward and to the right. As he does, take another step with your right foot and hammer his head or upper chest with your free right hand. Remember to lean your body forward coincident with the hammer.

7. To Cover (Kai) *(Figs. 175–190)*

FORM: Extend both arms forward, the left leading. Now bring them far to the rear as your left foot slides back slightly (in photo 177 the left foot should come back a bit more). Toeing out with your left foot, bring your right foot forward ahead of your left and on its toes while your right arm circles high and your left arm passes in front of your chest. Continuing, do a deep squat, with your right arm finally stopping in line with your shoulders.

FUNCTION: Your opponent uses his right fist. Capture his arm and pull it toward your right foot. As he resists, you follow him, stepping forward with your right foot and striking with your right

178

179

180

77

hand. Figures 188–90 show that the strike involves three impacts, (1) elbow, (2) palm-butt, and (3) fingers, and is accentuated by the squatting action.

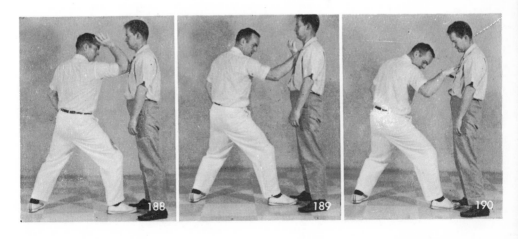

8. To Bind (Ch'an) *(Figs. 191–199)*

FORM: Turn your left toes out and scoop to your left with your left fist as you squat. Then take your right fist, palm up, forward from under your nose as your right foot goes forward. The intermediate step of your right foot on toes a little ahead of your left is not shown, but should not be neglected.

80

FUNCTION: This form can be used against either a foot or hand attack. Your opponent kicks at you with his right foot. Swinging leftward from your waist, deflect his foot outward in a circle and step forward on the toes of your right foot. Retaining your bar under his right foot, take your right fist forward with your right foot and attack his lower abdomen or groin. The final action is shown from both sides.

9. To Cut (Chieh) *(Figs. 200–207)*

FORM: Bring your left hand back in a fist to your right side in a downward rolling motion as you bring your left foot back on its toes. Your right fingers are open at your left elbow. As your left foot goes forward, reverse-punch toward your left with your left fist. Toe-out with your left foot, turn your left hand over, depress and punch over it with a standing right fist as your right foot goes directly forward.

FUNCTION: In this form the arms should not be held too high. Your

opponent tries a right fist which you deflect and grasp from outside with your right hand. As you pull him toward your right side, turn your waist to the right and lock his elbow with your roll. (In Fig. 205 the locking arm has curled after striking the elbow and is close to his wrist). Retaining your grip on his right wrist, step forward with your left foot and reverse punch his right chest with your left fist, which glides along the under surface of his arm to the target. If at this juncture he should strike with his left hand, depress it with your left and punch over it with your right standing fist.

10. To Conceal (Ts'ang) *(Figs. 208–214)*

FORM: Turn your left toes out and pull back to your left side with your left hand as your right hand circles high from left to right (clockwise). Continuing the circle, turn your palm up when your biceps are on a line with your shoulder. Simultaneously, your right foot comes forward on its toes, a fist-width ahead of your left. Next, push forward with your left hand under your right as your right foot goes forward.

FUNCTION: As your opponent strikes with his left fist, deflect and pull it toward your left side. In the same motion, wheel to the right from the waist and clamp your right hand under his nose (in clamping, *think* in and then up, not merely up, or you will lose him). As he raises his left elbow to take the clamp off, release the clamp and, turning clockwise, come under his rising left arm, grab his triceps and screw counterclockwise in a small circle. What should happen here is that, in his agony, he will strike with his right hand. If he does, depress with your left and hammer into his head with your

right as your right foot goes forward (this method is not shown). If he does not strike, step forward with your right as you strike his heart with your left hand from under your right, which continues the triceps pinch.

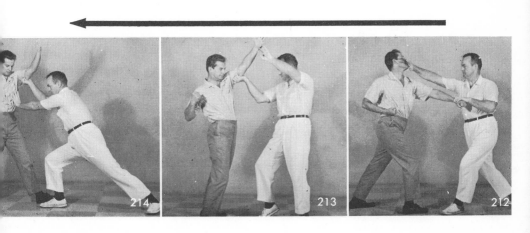

11. To Hack (K'an) *(Figs. 215–221)*

FORM: Here we put to use the *Hand Sword* (Exercise No. 1). Go forward with your right hand under your left elbow as your right foot goes behind your left. Then take your left foot forward as you begin to hack. Let your waist lead you!

FUNCTION: Your opponent grabs your left elbow in a defensive action. Step forward with your right foot behind your left foot and place your right forearm against your left triceps. Turning your right arm, grab his wrist and, retaining your hold, take your left foot forward and hack his throat with your left hand-edge.

12. TO SCRAPE (HSUEH) *(Figs. 222–230)*

FORM: Bring your right hand back slightly and toe-out your left foot. Swinging your arms in a counterclockwise circle, cut at 45°, your hands ending near your left foot and your right foot coming forward on its toes. Now, taking your right foot straight forward and then to the right (but aligned directly to the front), your right arm turns up to guard your forehead as your left palm pumps forward. Now, take your left foot straight ahead, then left, and put it down facing directly to the front. Roll your left arm up in front of your forehead and pump forward with your right palm.

FUNCTION: Deflect your opponent's right hand with your left to the left, come forward on your toes, and lock-strike his elbow. As he punches with his left, roll-deflect it upward with your right hand and hit him with your left palm as your right foot goes forward. He takes his right foot back and strikes with his right fist. Counter by taking a step forward with your left foot, rolling up with your right hand to deflect his right strike and palming his heart with your right hand. Don't deflect his punches too high: the closer he is, the better you can counter! As with most of the *Forms*, Scrape can be done as effectively against a leading left hand as against a right.

13. To Block (Lan) *(Figs. 231–237)*

FORM: Hammer with your left fist as you take a half-step with your left foot and toe-out. Bringing your right foot onto its toes in front of your left foot, take your right elbow high and your right hand to where it touches your left from underneath. Both palms are down. As you take a step forward with your right foot, push your right palm with your left hand.

FUNCTION: Your opponent has his left foot advanced and tries a left punch. Block his left from outside with your left hammer. Depress, and as he resists by raising his arm, step forward on the toes of your right foot and jam your left elbow *above* his elbow. Forcing his arm up, roll off; with your left arm, cover your right hand and, as you go forward with your right foot, pump your right hand with your left into his heart.

91

14. TO WALK (TSOU) *(Figs. 238–243)*

FORM: Take your left hand palm out and thumb down toward your left oblique as you toe-out with your left foot. Now, as your right foot goes forward to the left oblique, underspear with your right hand over your left hand and in the same direction as your right toes.

FUNCTION: Your opponent has his left foot forward and tries to hit you with his left fist. Block from outside with your left arm, overturn, and retain your hold. Step forward with your right foot as you spear over your descending left hand to his throat.

94

15. To Uphold (T'o) *(Figs. 244–250)*

FORM: Toe-out your left foot as your left hand circles clockwise with the fingers down. Then squat and put your left hand by your left foot, right hand lower and in front of it, as your right foot comes forward on its toes. Pull back with both your hands and then circle them high and forward (the left hand held high, the right medium) as your right foot goes forward.

FUNCTION: This is a defense against a kick. With his left foot forward, your opponent tries a right kick. Circle to the left from your waist, lower your body, and circle your left hand under his leg, deflecting and capturing it. Bringing your right foot forward on its toes, circle your right hand under his knee. Pull toward yourself with both hands and then continue the circle by stepping forward with your right foot and throwing your left hand high in the air. This really launches an antagonist into orbit, and during practice it may be well for the defender to do what the coward in Fig. 250 does—to hang on the attacker's head. In this way you work up repetitions without injury.

254 253

16. To Lower (Chui) *(Figs. 251–259)*

FORM: From the starting position, slide your left foot on its toes
back to your right foot while your hands clench into fists and your
left elbow raps down, your right fist close to it. Immediately step
up with your left foot and extend your left arm, the right fist still at
your left elbow. Now, roll your left arm back to guard your forehead as your right standing fist bangs forward with your right foot.
FUNCTION: This elbow technique may be used against foot or fist.
Your opponent tries to strike your chest with his right hand. Strike
the top of his fist with your left elbow and then the knuckles of

259

258

252   251

your fist in a double impact. Immediately step forward with your
left leg and attack his head with your extended left fist as your right
fist stays beside your left elbow. He withdraws his right hand and
strikes at your head. Roll your left hand back to your forehead,
deflecting his attack, and simultaneously step forward with your
right foot as you hit his chest with a standing punch. But, you say,
his right hand presumably is hurt by your left elbow—wouldn't he
be more apt to throw his left fist as a counter? And, if he did, what
would you do? For the answer see Fig. 259; merely roll your right
hand up and strike with your left as your right foot goes up.

257   256   255

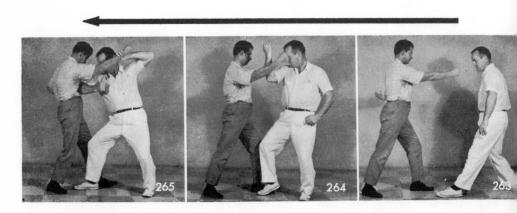

261 260

17. To Cross (Heng) *(Figs. 260–265)*

FORM: As your right foot comes forward on its toes, twist your right arm vertically in front of you (the biceps on a line with your shoulder). Now step to the right oblique with your right foot as, clenching your right fist, you elbow in the same direction. Your left hand is near your right.

FUNCTION: Your opponent has his left foot forward and strikes with his right fist. Step forward with your right foot on toes as you vertically block from inside with your right forearm. Now, stepping forward with your right foot, attack his chest with your right elbow. Fig. 265 shows your left hand capturing his right after the block. Although difficult, this is possible, but is only incidental to the action. You may add a movement by taking a short step forward with your right foot and, pivoting on your elbow, strike him with a right hammer.

18. To Seize (Lu) *(Figs. 266–272)*

FORM: Take your right foot to the right oblique as your right hand, palm up, sweeps in a big counterclockwise circle from right to left. Turn your right hand over so that the palm is down and continue the circle, now from left to right, and place your left foot on its toes in front of your right. Your two hands now nestle near your right side. From this corner, step forward with your left foot and push with both hands. This technique follows a zig-zag path.

FUNCTION: As your opponent strikes with his left fist, take your right foot obliquely right and block from outside with your circling right arm toward your left. At this point he counters with a right cross. Continuing your circle, you attack his right arm circularly from above and outside, rolling it toward your right side. Your left foot has come on its toes in front of your right. Next, step forward with your left foot and push his right external obliques with both hands.

19. Two (Erh) *(Figs. 273–284)*

FORM: Take a half-step with your left foot to the left oblique and toe-out. Now step forward with your right foot as your right hand, palm up, slices horizontally right to left and your left hand, palm down, pulls back to your left side in a near-fist. Toe-out with your right foot and go forward with your left foot and palm in the same way. Extend your hands over your head and pull down to your right foot as your left foot slides back on its toes in front of your right. As your left foot goes forward, push with both hands.

FUNCTION: Your opponent has his left foot forward and jabs with his left fist. Deflect the strike from outside with your left, secure a

hold, and carry it to the left toward your left side. At the same time, step up with your right foot (by this time it should not be necessary to tell you to toe-out with the left foot) and, swinging your right hand palm up, strike his side. He takes his right foot back and strikes with his right hand, which you deflect from outside with your right hand. Pull toward your right side as you toe-out with your right foot and go forward with your left hand and foot. Next, both hands reach up, grasp his right, and pull him sharply down toward your right foot. When he resists by rising, step forward with your left foot and push his midriff with both hands.

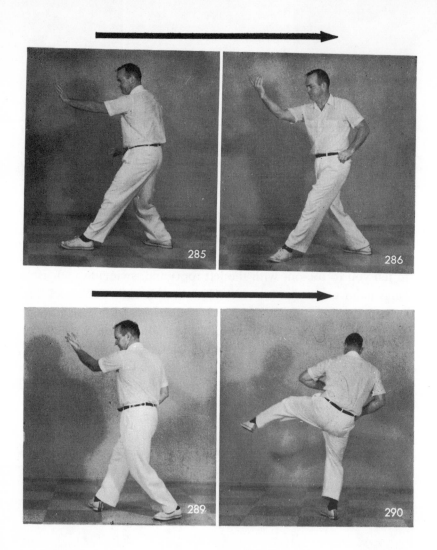

20. INWARD LEG HANGING (LI) *(Figs. 285–299)*

FORM: Toe-out with your left foot as you stab toward the left oblique with your right palm, pulling your left hand back to your left side in a fist. Now pull your right hand to your right side in a

fist as your right foot dashes forward *(Fig. 287)*. Put your right foot down toed-out, and stab toward the right oblique with your left palm. Pulling your left hand toward your left side, twirl to the right on your right foot, kicking (in passing) with your left. Con-

(Con't.)

tinue the 270° turn and end in a crouch, your arms close together.
Next, rise on your left foot and, as your arms open (your right
hammering forward), kick with your right heel.

FUNCTION: Your opponent has his left foot forward and strikes with
his right fist. *Cross* from outside with your right forearm, grasp,
and pull him toward your right side as your right foot dashes forward to hit his lower tibia (or, alternatively, strike his knee-cap
with either a toe-sole double impact stomp or simply a toe, Fig.
295). As you put your right foot down, he strikes with his left fist

106

which you *cross* with your left from outside. Securing his left arm, pull it toward your left side as you spin to the right on your right foot. The spin will take your left toes against the very sensitive inner surface of his knee-cap. Following through, complete your spin in a semi-squat. He steps forward with his right foot and raises his right fist. Rising, heel-kick his lower abdomen with your right foot and hammer either his head or his striking arm (whichever is most accessible) with your right arm. Although Pa-kua has some leg maneuvers (in Chang Chun-feng's method, 8 out of 64 basic postures were devoted to legs), it tends to downplay them. Leg techniques are only effective if (1) kept low, (2) done as a counter, and (3) done *only* when opponent's posture is broken. Even on two feet, man is essentially unstable. In kicking—because you stand on one leg—you add to this instability. It is mitigated somewhat if your kick is kept low and done only against an unbalanced opponent. Figures 300 and 301 show these requirements met in a kick which is near the height limit for safety. Here you are countering, seizing, pulling, and attacking. In this posture he has no return. The great prize here—the kidney: for no other reason should you go so high.

C. AFTERTHOUGHTS AND EXAMINATION

Eighteen *Exercises* and 20 *Forms* and *Functions* have been described and illustrated. How should they be practiced and learned? First, read the text, study it, sweat on it. This book was not meant to grace cork-lined studies; it is a workbook. So work with it! To learn this method I practiced in a casket factory, grocery store, and wherever else I could, under men who knew little Mandarin. I knew no Taiwanese, and so we were reduced to grunts. And still, I emerged with a fair hunk of the system. You have but the trouble of reading the text, comparing what you read with the photographs, and putting it to use.

Because the *Exercises* are independent actions done in many repetitions, they are not linked. Do them daily and in the doing learn the basics and perfect your character by overcoming the boredom forever dogging our days. The *Forms* are different; they are amenable to linkage, and this will make them easier to do. First off, though, learn all the *Forms* before practicing the uses. Do the *Forms*: (1) correctly, (2) speedily, and (3) lightly. Power will come as the bodily components merge into one and the movement makes the best use of that one. Don't force the exercise; better too light than too heavy. If you use strength instead of *ch'i*,* the vital force fashioning our existence, your movements will be ponderous and slow.

Learn the 20 *Forms* on both sides; that is, alternatively do them with your left foot forward and then, reversely, with your right foot forward. For example, do *Form* 1, which ends with your right palm thrusting forward over your right leg. Bring your left foot forward half the distance to your right, toe-out your right foot, depress with your right hand and do the posture from the right side. Left-right-left-right-left with *Form* 1 will suffice in one direc-

---

* See page 122 for further discussion of *ch'i*.

tion. Then you must turn and do *Form* 2. To make the turn (because you ended *Form* 1 with a left-side action, the right hand and foot ahead), simply turn leftward and come back whence you started with the five actions of *Form* 2, left, right, left, right, left.

When you have learned both sides of all 20 *Forms*, link them. In the linkage, do four *Forms* one way, turn, and do four *Forms* the other way. Whichever foot is forward do the *Form* from that side. For example, *Form* 1 finishes with your right foot advanced, so go into the right side of *Form* 2, which finishes with the right foot advanced, requiring you to do the right side of *Form* 3. This *Form* concludes with your left foot forward, so do *Form* 4 from the left side. *Form* 4 ends with your right foot forward, so turn leftward and begin *Form* 5, going the other way, from the left side. Do four *Forms* each way, and five times along the walk will let you do all 20 in under 3 minutes. In making a turn, if your right foot is advanced, turn leftward so your left foot is ahead. If your left foot is ahead, turn back rightward so your right foot is forward.

The following table shows the 20 *Forms* divided in five links and the side from which each is begun.

Link 1	Link 2	Link 3	Link 4	Link 5
1. Left	5. Left	9. Right	13. Left	17. Right
2. Right	6. Right	10. Left	14. Right	18. Left
3. Right	7. Left	11. Right	15. Left	19. Left
4. Left	8. Right	12. Right	16. Right	20. Left

When you have linked the 20 *Forms* and can run through them smoothly and correctly in the five links, begin practicing the uses. Here especially, work for speed and use the push—not the strike. If you can push your partner easily, think how much more punishing it would be were you striking. To practice the strikes use auxiliary equipment: a heavy bag, a punching post (the Japanese *makiwara*), or your partner's shoulders. Using the shoulder as a punching bag, however, is not without its dangers. It was Hung I-hsiang's delight—particularly on those nights when wine had been imbibed—to "illustrate" punches on my shoulders. A recurrent bursitis has resided there since. This digression is useful only as it pertains to pain. Regular practice will raise your pain threshold. Irrespective of this, your practice should always be focused on correct technique done speedily and gracefully. To end this section and to fix the vitals of the method solidly in your mind, try to answer the following questions.

1. When and why must one toe-out?

2. Should one try to develop a very speedy and high kick?

3. Look at Form 1. At what stage could your head be used with good effect?

4. See Figs. 302–303. Which is better in the final action of the *Forms*, to stay extended or to follow-step with the rear foot half the distance to the front foot?

5. Look at Figs. 304 through 307. Can you figure out the function of this *Form?* If you score well (and it is tough), you are well on your way to creating your own *kua*. Beyond that, the ulti-

mate good is to dispense entirely with method. Absorb the principles, learn the tactics, and then forget all. This sounds paradoxical and is merely bait for the next section.

1. You must toe-out the lead foot when you intend to step over and off it. Test yourself: keep your toes straight and stand on one leg. Now toe-out and stand. Stability is enhanced greatly by this move. An additional point: when kicking, *always* toe-out. Otherwise you will wobble.

2. No, unless he plays football.

3. As you bring your right foot forward on its toes while depressing his right hand with your left, *fake* with your head toward his head. This will cause him to jerk his head back, opening his body for your strike-push.

4. See Figs. 302–303. Either is correct. Initially, it is best to stay extended so as not to shortchange the technique. Later, use the follow-step. In order to link one technique with another the follow-step must be used.

5. See Figs. 304–307. Catch his striking left fist from outside with your left and use your right arm in a lock-strike against his left elbow. Then hammer-strike with your right fist as your right foot comes forward on its toes. He deflects your hammer with his right arm. Turn your right arm counterclockwise under and out, grabbing his right elbow. As you go forward with your right foot, palm with your left hand under your right.

III
The Classical Circling Exercise and Its Modifications

THE GULF between what you have just learned and classical Pa-kua is quite wide. These exercises, with their emphasis on the linear rather than the circular, are akin in this respect to *Hsing-i*. It is said that Pa-kua employs chiefly *horizontal* strength and *hsing-i, vertical* strength. If I attack you on a straight line with body and legs advancing, that is *vertical* strength. But if I intercept your arm laterally and attack on a curving line with my body rotating, that is *horizontal* strength. There is a good deal of vertical strength in the beginning method and considerably less in the classical. The former may be thought of as a linear method containing circles and the latter as a dynamic circular method. The linear is only a part of Pa-kua, while the circular is the whole.

To set the stage for the classical system, I use the notes presented to me by Kuo Feng-ch'ih, my instructor for more than two years. I have edited out some repetition, but otherwise the notes are as he wrote them. As in love, the preliminaries to an *Internal* boxing method are vitally important. Therefore, pay close attention. The thoughts expressed govern all three *Internal* methods. Thus if you understand these ideas, you comprehend the rationale of *T'ai-chi* and *Hsing-i*, as well as Pa-kua.

A. KUO FENG-CH'IH'S ADVICE

One month has passed since I began teaching you Pa-kua. We have met two or three times a week for an hour each session. Although you have tried diligently, your progress is slow because you have not conformed to the requirements for an *Internal* learner. You lack the concept of the *Internal (nei chia)*. You can get it through ridding yourself of erroneous but ingrained thoughts, and through substituting somewhat revolutionary and scientific ideas. With this goal and with perseverance and humility, you can master Pa-kua.

1. RELAXATION AND SLOWNESS

In *Internal Boxing* the beginning step is to gain a foothold *(chan chuang)*; that is, to take a standing posture in which the novice may quiet his nerves and relax and soften his muscles. This phase is largely mental, almost spiritual, and says that the mind can will relaxation and softness. As you stand, you practice this willing of the tranquil flow from your eyebrows to the soles of your feet. Your mind thus travels this imagined route. With practice and concentration all distracting thoughts will be shut out, your nerve-ends sharpened but at ease, and your whole being peaceful and sublimated. Thus your mind is liberated, and, when this happens, your body and limbs will attain a happy, unencumbered circulation of air and blood.

Chan chuang is literally a maneuvering of the mind for gaining a static outside and a dynamic inside. Chinese philosophy of ancient vintage says: "To stand still results in the mind's settlement, mind's settlement in tranquility, tranquility in a sense of security, security in wholesome thinking, and wholesome thinking in great accomplishment." The ancients followed this philosophy to cultivate their bodies as well as their minds.

The word *slowness* refers not only to action but also to a state of mind free from any impatience and anxiety. Haste seldom solves anything. Slowness therefore is needed to alleviate the tense desire for progress and success. Slowness harmonizes the outside and inside influences. By beginning slowly the novice will have sufficient time to *seek, listen to, feel for*, and apprehend the quintessence of boxing and to adjust his body and limbs to test the reactions from the various muscles. This will increase his potential as a novice boxer.

These are secrets of the *Internal* system. Traditionally, secrets are not disclosed casually. In fact, the so-called secrets are not really very secret. Most secrets lie in what occurs in our everyday life, in our being most natural. But because they are posited on an ordinary base, people usually ignore them. *Internal Boxing* does not.

2. The Mind (I)

The mind *(i)* in Chinese is usually synonymous with the heart *(hsin)*. According to Chinese psychology, the mind dominates all actions. *Internal Boxing* insists that three things are coordinated: "The mind *(i)* commands, strength *(li)* goes along, and vital energy *(ch'i)* follows." Consciously or subconsciously all physical functions are directed by the mind. Training the mind slowly enables one to transform internal truths into external boxing forms. But it must be done slowly. If a beginner lays too much stress on physical performance, he will fall short. How important the concept of mind is to boxing may be seen in the very names of the three orthodox *Internal* systems: *t'ai-chi* (The Great Ultimate), *hsing-i* (The Form of Mind), and Pa-kua (The Eight Diagrams), all suggesting thought and action in unison.

3. Breathing

During practice the novice invariably pants and has difficulty breathing. *Internal Boxing* will overcome this by teaching you to "sink" your breath to your navel, which will permit you to breathe normally even in the midst of strenuous movement. Practice itself will harmonize action and breathing. One sees this in almost any sport—from swimming to track. To adjust one's breathing is to regularize it in time to slow or fast movement. While eating, without being conscious of it, we continually adjust our breathing. This is truly natural and the thing to be strived for in boxing. The novice should not fuss about breathing; gradually and naturally it will take care of itself. The *Internal* stresses naturalness and often uses the analogy of a child. Watch how a child breathes and then do likewise.

4. The Use of Strength

Some boxing masters have said that it is not right to use strength, nor is it right not to use strength. This seeming paradox may be explained in this way. The central idea is *how* to use your strength at a given time. A novice thinks that the increase of strength depends on the use of strength—that is, you cannot lift a heavy weight without using strength. Correct, but strength and the function of strength are different things. The strength of the so-called muscle man or weight lifter is entirely different from the strength of *Internal Boxing*. Our strength is reserved inside and evenly distributed. It is always living and highly volatile. When held in reserve it gives one a high-spirited appearance and when released it fairly radiates. This kind of strength means much more than the kind employed to lift a weight or to hurt an enemy.

It is easier for a weak person or one who knows nothing of boxing to learn the *Internal* methods. Such a person is not preoccupied with past instruction and has no reservation on the advice given. He merely goes ahead and follows it. Boxing masters instruct their students to learn boxing by following the three requirements mentioned above:

Softness (relaxation)

Slowness (prolongation of posture)

Evenness (of actions and breathing)

With these mastered, a promising embryo for learning *Internal Boxing* is formed.

5. SUBSTANCE AND FUNCTION

To eradicate erroneous ideas you may have, I desire to draw a comparison between the *Internal* and *External* types of boxing. Based on an analysis of substance and function there is a remarkable difference between the two arts. The *Internal* is based on the combined training of spirit and body, exemplified in the doctrines of Buddhism and Taoism. The main goal of these doctrines is to achieve the state of holding a "great air" without any worldly desire or bellicose attitude, neither humble nor arrogant, always advancing and indomitable. "Spiritual" cultivation in *Internal Boxing* is given top priority, but boxing theory and practice must also be accorded their due. When you box, the "spiritual" cultivation is transformed into physical activity in exactly the right proportion required for the work at hand.

External Boxing, on the other hand, stresses the physical or material side. It stresses external muscle size and achievement and pragmatic postures. It likes the flamboyant display, the demonstration of strength. Visually, the two appear similar to the layman, whereas, actually, they are quite remote from each other. First, muscle training in *External Boxing* is restricted by age, whereas the mental cultivation of *Internal Boxing* continues through life and, if

117

anything, becomes more profound at an advanced age. Undeniably the use of a single part of the body in *External Boxing* is often admirable. But this requires time, effort, and strength, and the gain made often leaves other parts of the body defenseless. The strength of *Internal Boxing*, however, is hidden inside and permeates everywhere in equal proportions. Reserved inside, it is virtually inexhaustible and can be gathered for use. Permeating the whole body, the strength of the *Internal* is not localized and can shoot forth from any quarter. It can be hard or soft, cover a wide area or a small spot, and be drawn for use externally or reserved inside.

In actual boxing there are many other differences between the two in respect to principles and methods. The *Internal* studies the theory of *change*, and the interplay of *yin* (soft) and *yang* (hard), and how to win by wisdom rather than tricks. Its desire is to win without a hot fight (economically), but to win so that no doubt lingers in the mind of the attacker (efficiently). An *Internal Boxing* master can dodge, deflect, and counterattack instinctively because the mental training has made him both efficient and economical.

An ancient boxing classic states: "Boxing is like taking a walk; striking an enemy is like snapping your fingers." The *External* cares only for demonstrable skills, whereas the *Internal* reserves and does not demonstrate its skills, which, if anything, have been more scientifically developed than those of the *External*. In sum, the substance and function of the two systems are entirely different. The substance of *Internal Boxing* is on the mental, not the material, level, and its function is not limited to the mere performance of boxing. It brings health with it and, therefore, can be said to teach fighting and living skills at the same time.

6. CONCEPTS NEEDED FOR TRAINING

The novice needs a firm will and perfect confidence to understand and appreciate the function of *Internal Boxing*. He must prepare himself mentally and must have the correct concepts in mind. A beginner is like a man going on a trip. If he wants to reach his destination quickly and safely, he will select the best means and the shortest route.

The ideal student is one of middle age because he accumulates knowledge and experience as he matures. Confucius said, "A person at forty will not be diverted." This originally referred to ethical cultivation, but can be applied to any kind of learning. When young, a person tends to show off strength, but when he is old his strength will fail him. Then he knows that what he had earlier was superficial and of no use. Guilt and regret then impel him to learn the art from the start. A person with such an awakening is very likely to progress rapidly. He now is quiet and receptive and his psychology is correct. He turns his personal and sensual desires to the spiritual side. In this way he becomes tranquil. He then assesses things properly and is always calm. Then he starts learning. *Internal Boxing* doctrine says that *wu-wei* (doing nothing that is not natural or spontaneous) is required. *Wu-wei* is to become like a blank piece of paper. Every *Internal* student tries to achieve this. It brings harmony to his life. This process, however, requires time and energy.

Wrong ideas can put the student on the wrong track—examples are numerous. Some divide the *Internal* into *hard, soft*, and *change*, equating the *hard* to *hsing-i*, the *soft* to *t'ai-chi*, and the *change* to Pa-kua. Some also say that *hsing-i* is for youngsters, Pa-kua for the middle-aged, and *t'ai-chi* for oldsters. How absurd! *Internal* experts used to say that the three have the same end, yet employ different means. This statement must not be interpreted as a relay race but rather like three links in a chain of command to

119

attain an end. From *hsing-i*, you can learn the physical aspects of the *Internal* function. From *t'ai-chi* and Pa-kua you can reach the spiritual phenomenon of *Internal Boxing*. The relay race analogy was taught by some quack boxers. If you believe it you will never enter the gate of *Internal Boxing* even if you practice all your life.

To go further, the three arts suggest a correct basis for learning boxing. They stress *i* (mind). From *i*, action comes and is dominated. The idea is to keep still although your body moves. That is *i*. To remain still although the body turns circularly—that is Pa-kua, and to do so while the body goes in a straight line—that is *hsing-i*. The idea is formed, and if you want to move, you do; if you want to stay still, you do. If you want to be hard or soft, you will it. This emptied aspect brings transformation. Any of the three arts can bring it. Also, all three can at different times be hard or soft. It is entirely wrong to say that one is soft and the other hard. Soft and hard in boxing are transitional phases.

To learn the *Internal*, the spirit must dominate the body. At first adopt *wu-wei* and *wang-o* (forgetting self). This is the spiritual construction of a foundation. Then accept these basic but radical ideas:

(1) Boxing requires movement but first the *Internal* requires stillness;

(2) To defeat the enemy requires strength, but first the *Internal* requires softness;

(3) Fighting requires speed, but first the *Internal* requires slowness.

If a person desires to learn *Internal Boxing* with the maximum speed and the greatest efficiency, he has to heed all the above. To achieve the apex of boxing these three basic ideas are the best transport for your voyage. If a boxer cannot accept these ideas he is not qualified to learn *Internal Boxing*. Thus *Internal* boxers put students into two categories.

120

1. *To know first, to act second.* Which means that before you act you learn step by step with great deliberation. With this temperament, it is easy for such a student to learn *Internal Boxing.* When he learns one technique he can develop it to 10. Even with no teacher the achievement of such students will be great and they can attain their goal.

2. *To act without knowing.* These students learn everything the teacher shows by rote, mechanically, without asking *how* or *why.* Their achievement will not be great.

7. A FINAL WORD

For your body to accept the gift of this art it must not only be disciplined but also must literally be remade. By endeavoring to subtract the antagonisms, spasms, and clumsy habits accumulated since birth, we are able to achieve a "pre-birth" (that is, a natural) body. This is a body capable of being molded correctly. It involves initially relaxation and softness, from which later springs true hardness. Do the exercises slowly so as to enhance feeling. Think and feel mightily as you do the movement. Pause at the end of the movement—inaction often aids relaxation. The more you relax in the first phase, the more strength you will have in the second.

Sun Lu-t'ang made much of the proper balance between pre- and post-birth strength. The shapeless movement in boxing we call natural or "pre-birth." Shaped movement, such as that of the hand, foot, or body, we call "post-birth." The two must be coordinated. Think of *ch'i* as the feeling, rather than the breath. Centered in the navel, it should have a feeling of "bursting up." If the exercises are done correctly, you cannot but feel the *ch'i* permeate your body, enhance your boxing, and change your life. The first phase of training may be summarized as follows:

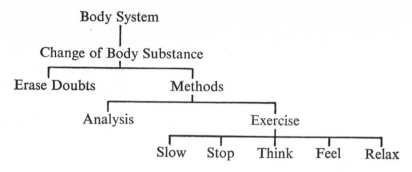

Now for the second phase. Say that you have succeeded in co-ordinating mind and action, spiritual and material, substance and function. Now you must do more about real boxing and its creation. The entrance to the second phase is made when wasteful strength is eschewed by your being able to adjust your body automatically without extra commands. The subconscious takes over. Your body is permeated by a warm air. Your hair pores feel as if they were opening; your sides and your fingertips feel extraordinarily strong. You are now approaching the level when you can spontaneously counter an enemy. Imagine enemies pressing you from all sides. You must use your totality to counter them. This involves shouting to dishearten the enemy.

When you have acquired a strong body through Pa-kua, you must use soft strength with it. This means the avoidance of rigid, tense postures and actions. Stay relaxed until the moment of impact with your opponent. I call it the refining of steel. Getting powerful strength is akin to making iron: steel can be made just as durable but soft. When you have powerful strength it is used without control. But the soft helps to manage the hard. It guides the *ch'i* to the navel where it is stored. Ultimately your lower navel will swell. This is caused by air circulation and is the harbinger of excellence in boxing. The hard *(yang)* and soft *(yin)* are coordinated and meshed so well that one always accompanies the other

122

instead of their being separate contrasts. They are harmonized so that if one uses too much "hard," automatic adjustment is made and the soft comes forward to even the balance. When you have this you have achieved *I-ch'i* (the one *ch'i*; your body and the universe are one).

Is this enough? No, you must go further. Check your actions. Aim for the proper action at the right time. You always remain calm, but your action explodes and is irresistible. The action disturbs not the calmness. This is the ultimate, but it is within your grasp. It depends on how hard you work.

B. THE MAIN PRINCIPLES

Pa-kua is not easy. Although it can be learned in less time than the two decades the old masters insisted on, it still requires regular and tedious practice over a period of several years.

Chou Chi-ch'un, one of the leading historians of Chinese boxing, once told me:

> Pa-kua is difficult to learn. You walk slowly for two or three years, then go faster and, later, very fast.* The chief aims are to move behind an opponent quickly and to strengthen your arms. Through the practice, heavy weights later can be attached to your arms without discomfort. At the turn of the century a famous master went to Japan and, while there, supported the weight of a sumo wrestler on his outstretched arm! Often, accomplished boxers while spinning and turning their bodies rapidly would carry a cup of tea in each palm without spilling a drop!

The most important principles of Pa-kua are as follows:

---

* Some of the old masters circled so swiftly that their queues stood out horizontally as they moved.

1. *Move your body naturally.* The best rule for this is to follow all the rules. Avoid the rudimentary shao-lin and karate movements. They are woodenly rigorous and exhausting.

2. *Stretch your arm but withdraw your trapezius muscles.* (This is only one example of the apparently antagonistic actions implicit .n Pa-kua.) Another is to lower your waist by "feeling" downward the small of the back muscles while your sacrum feels as if it will spring up.

3. *Harmonize your vital energy and your strength.* Read again Kuo Feng-ch'ih's remarks on this.

4. *Keep your vital energy concentrated below your navel.* This refers to the psychic energy center, roughly three inches below your navel, where your center of gravity is also to be found. Physiologically, this means to "sink" your strength from the upper to the lower torso to gain stability.

C. OTHER PRINCIPLES TO MASTER

1. Keep your chest depressed, not arched, so that your *ch'i* can circulate.

2. Hold the tip of your tongue on your hard palate (the roof of the mouth) and hold your head straight (as if carrying a cup of tea on it).

3. Expand or open your back by rounding your shoulders and dropping them so they are not prominent.

4. Hang your elbows down with strength when extending or twisting your arms.

5. Master the technique of:
   a. Rise *(ch'i)* —start to raise your hand.
   b. Drill *(tsuan)*—as it ascends, turn the palm upward in a clockwise drilling strike.
   c. Fall *(lo)* —begin to lower your hand, palm still up.

124

d. Overturn *(fan)*—as it descends, twist the right palm
   downward in a counterclockwise strike or grasp.
This is done as one action, and the great masters could do it like
lightning. This action can be seen in Figs. 6–9.

D. THINGS TO AVOID
The student should avoid three things:

1. *Breathing strain.* Breathe naturally. Do not hold your
breath. This brings exhaustion.

2. *Too much strength.* This is usually the cause of breathing
strain (1, above). If you tighten your muscles, it impedes inner
health and outer pliability. It is doubly detrimental in that it is
unnecessary. Stay relaxed!

3. *Arching the chest.* In the West the large chest, arched to the
fullest, is considered the epitome of vital health. The strength
should be lowered to the lower torso, breathing should be deep
abdominal breathing rather than the shallow intercostal type, and
your mind should concentrate on your lower navel. None of these
can be done if you arch your chest. You will be unstable and un-
coordinated if you do.

E. TO "FEEL"
This is an important concept in Pa-kua. The mind is intensively
employed and the muscles actively engaged at every stage. To the
extent that the muscles are used properly, there should be a same-
ness in what you feel. But because the mind is an indispensable
ingredient in the process, the feeling one person may have (or
evaluate himself as having) as against the feeling another might
have may be quite different. Where the mind works there will always be a subjective element present. Irrespective of the nuances

you may feel, you must have the desire to feel and the faith to continue. As you feel, in like measure you will be forgotten. By hyperconcentration on the *me*, the *I* is forgotten. Thus, yogic-like, the art of Pa-kua aims to make the individual one with the universe. He tunes in through the postures and in the end is himself attuned.*

F. THE CONCEPT OF THE CIRCLE

The essence of Pa-kua is in the circling movement and its changes. To circle means to "walk the circle" and periodically to change directions. In this section we will contrast the classic circling style with the more recent modifications. The reader thus is free to choose which method he prefers. The classic style is that taught by Sun Lu-t'ang in his *Pa-kua Ch'uan Hsueh*.

Initially, in China the novice walked the circle for an hour a day. Although the knees must be well bent before mastery comes, at first bend them only within the confines of comfort. Even this will tire you—an hour of Pa-kua walking equates to at least an hour of the most strenuous sport known to man. This is because of the many technical points you must remember and because of the intense demands made on the mind.

The turning variations in Pa-kua are many *(see Fig. 308)*. First, your body turns by walking in one direction while the waist turns in the opposite direction. Your arms move directionally with the momentum of your body and push outward from the elbows, but, simultaneously, both have "pullback" energy originating from the trapezius muscles. As one arm attacks or deflects circularly out-

---

* Kuo Feng-ch'ih once told me that he and a friend in Tientsin often would practice blindfolded for hours. When one signaled in his mind that they should halt practice for the day, the other got the message and they stopped at the same time.

126

308

ward from your body, the other circles inward toward your body. Finally, amidst all these circles, your arms twist or turn independently in moving. The reason for all these circles? Circularity imparts speed and power to your actions.

In walking the circle we encounter a problem immediately. The ultimate aim is to enable the body to move, act, and react naturally. But initially we force ourselves into postures uncomfortable and unnatural. The body must be prepared and educated to the natural by methods which may seem unnatural. The classics say this: "from the unnatural to the natural" or "from the hard to the soft." In order to respond quickly one must be relaxed (soft). But for the tactic to be correct, the center of gravity low, the knees bent, we must first get into tiring, uncomfortable postures. These are unnatural because they hurt, but they are meant to undo habitually incorrect body attitudes. Once the forms are learned, the pain disappears and you are ready for whatever comes. This is a path which must be followed if the body is to react to external stimuli speedily and efficiently.

127

It comes down to the fact that in the beginning Pa-kua will seem the antithesis of the relaxed and natural boxing it is said to be. Paradoxically, once the postures are learned the student does become more adroit, relaxed, pliable, and powerful than even the most optimistic might imagine.

In circling, keep your knees bent and let your ankles touch as you walk. At first go very slowly and bring your rear foot suspended to your front ankle. After a slight pause, take the suspended foot forward and put it down. The orthodox school (Sun and most others) walked with feet separated and did not touch the ankles in advancing. Initially, the present method has the virtue of slowing the student down and makes for better stability. For these reasons I advocate it at least as a beginning method. Later, you may wish to follow Sun. As you put your foot down, touch the heel first and then let the rest of the sole fall gradually (this tentativeness is seen in all the *Internal* methods and is functionally fine—if the entire sole were placed down at once, an opponent could scoop your foot easily). The toes may be pointed in three ways: (1) directly ahead in a natural step, (2) in *k'ou*—that is, to turn your toes *inward* as you advance your outside foot; here the toes may touch first, and (3) in *pai*—that is, to turn your toes *outward*. If your right arm is extended in the circle you will be walking clockwise and your right foot will be inside. Your right foot has to *pai* (toe-out) each step in order to maintain the circle. If your left hand is in the center, you will be walking counterclockwise and your left foot, which is always inside (closest to the center), must toe-out to maintain the circle. On a small circle, your toe-out will be considerable and on a large one it will be barely discernible.

The size of the circle and the number of times you circle depends on the terrain and your own inclination. Initially, a circle with a diameter of approximately six feet is desirable. Later, you can circle a huge field or turn almost into yourself; wherever there is room for your two feet, you have room to circle. As you circle it is important to imagine an enemy following you.

This practice teaches you to walk without dizziness for long periods on circles of various sizes. While walking, it teaches you how to "circularize" your body so that other circles are added to the process. These circles, turns, and twists are done to make of your body one unit so that, if an opponent strikes, it takes an instant to defend and counterattack him.

After you have practiced the various postures on clockwise and counterclockwise circles of varying sizes, walk a figure 8 between two stations *(see Fig. 309)*. When this is mastered, walk through a series of nine in three tiers of three each, circling each station *(see Fig. 310)*. Go in both directions and arbitrarily use whatever posture you wish, but always feel the presence of an enemy. These circles add variety, but the actions remain the same.

If you slowly circle an hour a day, six days a week, you should recognize these changes in yourself within a month.

> You are more stable, you do not wobble; your strength has descended to your lower torso.

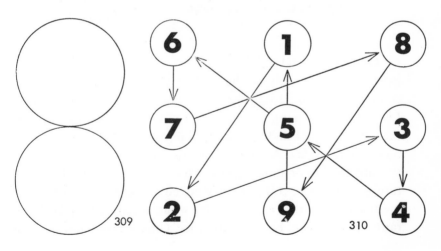

309

310

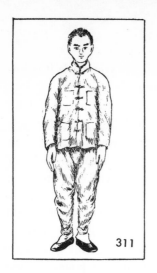

Your breathing is easier and you feel less tired.

You begin to feel the *ch'i* in your arms (the physical sensation is similar to the tingling experienced when one of your limbs "goes to sleep").

The stiffness which at first attacked your lower back has eased, bringing extreme suppleness.

G. QUIET STANDING

Before and after walking the circle it is well to stand quietly and compose yourself. Hold your head straight and your body upright. Let your hands hang naturally and put your heels together with the toes separated slightly. Empty your mind of thought. Your eyes do not stare. Relax! After some practice you will not know whether you are moving or standing still. This is the *wu-chih* (infinity) posture of Sun *(Fig. 311)*. Kuo Feng-ch'ih liked this posture and modified it slightly *(Fig. 312)*. He would separate his feet slightly rather than having his heels together. Once relaxed and the mind

130

tranquil, he would let his body spasmodically tremble in the manner of a horse. This can be done naturally only if the body is relaxed.

H. BEGINNING TO MOVE*

Take your left leg forward so that the left knee and heel are on a vertical line. Now raise your left hand in a semicircle to eye-level and your right hand near your left elbow. Relax your waist, and hang (point) your elbows down. Your left index finger stands vertically. Your "tiger mouth" (*hu k'ou*—that area of the hand from the tip of the thumb to the tip of the index finger) is opened like a crescent and pushes forward slightly. Bend the tips of your little fingers and ring fingers, hooking them downward. As you hold your palms away from you, you must *feel* that they are trying to turn inward toward you (the wrists are turning upward). The main strength of your left arm is contracted or withdrawn, and that of your rear hand is pushing outward and expanding. These tendencies must be differentiated and balanced. Throughout the action you gaze at the index finger of your left hand.

In contracting your trapezius muscles your right arm should be close to your body. Your back should be slightly bowed forward and tight as a drum. Your right "tiger mouth" is held near your left elbow. Both shoulders contract and both elbows point down. As your palms turn, imagine some resistance. While circling, your waist turns in the opposite direction of your hands—like twisting a rope. As you walk, the back of your thighs contract upward toward your sacrum; and your inner thighs contract both inward and upward toward your groin *(see again Fig. 308)*. Your head is up-

---

* In this section I have purposely repeated some of the material in Section F in order to emphasize certain vital fundamentals.

right, your mouth relaxed ("a little opened, a little closed"), and you breathe through your nose.

Hold your head level as though there were a weight on it. Walk slowly. To progress you must sink your *ch'i* to the navel. In turning, the level of your body must remain the same, always well balanced. Your shoulders likewise should remain on the same line. There must be a unity of the mind-vital energy-strength as well as of the body components, a unity both inside and outside the body which forms a total feeling embracing all the different feelings. This is done without dissipation of energy and in the end comes without conscious intent.

I. SINGLE PALM CHANGE (TAN HUAN CHANG)*

The main offensive action of Pa-kua is the *Single Change*. Indeed, it is more than that—it is the basic action in the art.

Extend your left hand into the center and step ahead with your left foot *(Fig. 313)*. Bring your right foot forward and toe-in near your left foot, about three to six inches separating the toes *(Fig. 314)*. Your heels feel as though they are turning outward and your knees almost touch. Your inner thighs turn inward and your outer thighs contract toward your sacrum. Your waist sinks and your upper torso remains steady. Your trapezius muscles contract.

Next, twist your left wrist downward until your thumb is down. Simultaneously, step forward with your left foot until it is vertically and directionally aligned with your left hand. Your right palm continues to push forward forcefully *(Fig. 315)*. Now take your right foot forward and toe-in near your left. Your back is now facing the center *(Fig. 316)*. Again, your heels feel as if they are twisting outward and your inner thighs contract with strength.

---

* Hereafter called simply *Single Change*.

132

Gradually twist your hands until both palms face up and, as you do, your shoulders contract with strength. Keep your waist going to the left as though twisting a rope. Your left elbow points down and, in turning, your right hand gradually passes under it. Hold your head upright and keep it coordinated with your waist. Gaze at your right hand, which stretches as far as it can. Go slowly! Keep a relaxed inside and this external action will not leave an opening for an attack.

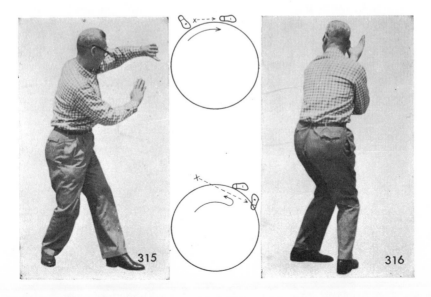

317 318 319

Turn slowly to the right *(Fig. 317)* and step out with your right foot. Twisting your right hand from under your left arm gradually as you circle, stretch it until your right index finger is perpendicular and the palm toward the center. Until your torso faces the center of the circle, keep your palms up and elbows down as you swing right *(Fig. 318)*. Finally, twist both of your palms down. Gaze at your right index finger; your right "tiger mouth" pushes forward; and your shoulders contract slightly.

To go the opposite way, simply reverse the procedure. Turn naturally, keeping the upper and lower body coordinated.*

The *Single Change* given above is that of Sun Lu-t'ang. It has been modified considerably since his time. Because of its stress on

---

* Your inside and outside points must be coordinated in terms of the six combinations, as follows:

Inner	*Outer*
heart/mind	shoulder/thigh
mind/vital energy	elbow/knee
vital energy/strength	hand/foot

320   321   322

slowness, however, it is the best method for a novice to practice in the beginning.

Now, let us look at the main variation. Start with your left palm extended and your left foot ahead *(Fig. 319)*. Toe-in your right foot beside your left foot *(Figs. 320–322)* and then step out with your left foot as your right hand continues to twist under your left *(Figs. 323–326)*. Finally, bring your right foot up and leave it suspended but touching your left ankle *(Figs. 327–329)*. After you have stretched your right arm under your left elbow to the left as far as you can, begin swinging back to the right and put your right foot down *(Figs. 330–333)*. Carrying your right arm circularly under your left, after about a circle's walk you should have the right palm in the center and the index finger vertical *(Fig. 334)*. Note that in Fig. 329 the left foot is different and it is wrong. This photograph was used to show the suspended right foot and the twisting upper torso.

135

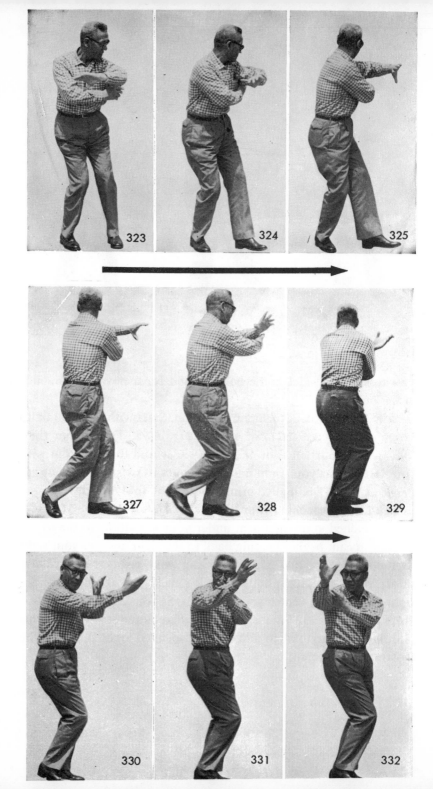

326

How is the modification different from Sun's? The change is more fluid and without the interruptions caused by extending the left arm and following into the second toe-in. In the modification, instead of extending the left arm you immediately "wrap" under it and, instead of the final toe-in, you bring your right foot to the left ankle suspended, which permits a somewhat faster swing back.

A further modification can be glimpsed in the style of Wang Shu-chin. On the final turn back from the suspended foot, instead of placing the right foot down immediately, he curves it in a circle upward and then down *(Figs. 335–337).*

What is the function of the *Single Change*? Kuo always took pains to state that it did not mean that you hit your enemy in a specific way. Rather it was a change permitting a rapid transition to another direction, which, if perfected, would make your response to an alien action a reflex not susceptible to analysis of how one did it. But if the reader still desires an explicit use, think simply

333

334

137

335   336   337

that an enemy attacks you from the center with his left fist. You
deflect from outside with your left hand as you toe-in your right
foot near your left foot. Turning leftward, take your left foot forward as you maintain pressure with your deflecting left palm.
Finally, spear his left side with your right palm as your right foot
goes forward to either toe-in (as in the Sun style) or to be held
suspended at the left ankle (as in the modification). From here, the
swing back to the right can be to handle his right, if he is able to
use it, or simply to address another attacker. Wang's rising right
foot on the swing back is used to deflect an opponent's leg attack.

J. DOUBLE PALM CHANGE (SHUANG HUAN CHANG)*

Again we will start with the Sun method and then move to the later modifications. Start with your left hand extended and turn the circle counterclockwise (Fig. 338). Toe-in your right foot near your left (Fig. 339). You are but half-centered now. Now toe-out your left foot (Kuo is stressing this by pointing in Fig. 340) as you turn your left thumb down and extend your left arm. Keep your waist going leftward coordinated with your left hand. Toe-in your right foot beside your left foot with your back to the center (Fig. 341) and twist your hands until the palms face up. Your right forearm turns under your left elbow. Again, toe-out your left foot and toe-in near it with your right foot. Your body now faces the center (Fig. 342). As you turn your left hand circularly downward to your left side and your right hand above your head, take your left foot off the ground and rise on your right foot (Fig. 343). Next, step to the left with your left foot in a natural step to nearly form a horse-riding posture (ma pu) as your arms are brought above and outside your thighs with the palms down (Fig. 344). Although your body is still centered, your head is twisted to the left and you gaze at your left hand. Toe-in your right foot near your left foot again and twist both palms up, your right hand again twisting under your left elbow (Fig. 345). Your back is toward the center. Now swing slowly rightward and begin to walk (Figs. 346–347). Your right hand gradually stretches into the center as both palms twist until they face downward (Figs. 348–349).

Now, the modifications. Practice Sun's basic style and only after mastering it change to the modifications. With your left hand extended walk the circle (Fig. 350). Toe-in your right foot as your left arm wipes downward past your right (Figs. 351–352). As you

* Hereafter called simply *Double Change*.

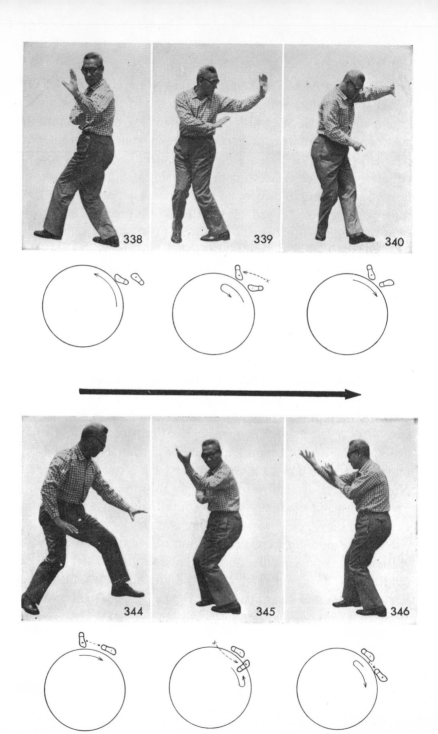

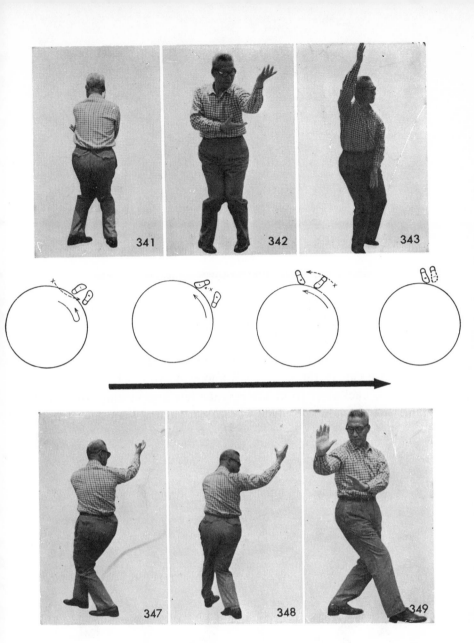

341 342 343

347 348 349

141

take your left hand palm up over your right, toe-out your left foot *(Fig. 354)*. Go forward and toe-in your right foot as your right arm stretches to its fullest extent *(Fig. 355)*. Your back is to the center. Next move your left foot backward and turn the toes as far as you can to the left. Simultaneously, your left hand twists, palm up, backward from under your left armpit and your right hand twists, palm up, backward from under your left armpit

and your right hand lowers to shoulder level *(Figs. 355–356)*. Now as you again twist your right arm under your left triceps *(Fig. 357–358)*, take your right foot up to your left and suspend it at the ankle, while your torso stretches leftward. Finally, swing back to the right and stretch your right hand into the center gradually as you walk *(Figs. 359–360)*.

The last modification of the *Double Change* is nearly like the first and is a style taught by Huang Po-nien in his *Lung Hsing Pa-kua Chang*. Kuo Feng-ch'ih illustrates it fully here. The only difference is that Huang's circle is tighter and the action more compressed. Start with your left palm extended *(Fig. 361)*. Toe-in your right foot to your left *(Figs. 362–365)* and then imitate the action illustrated in Figs. 366–376. You end up swinging to the right with your right palm extended.

After doing the exercises in Part II you should have no difficulty in ascertaining the function of the *Double Change*. Indeed, it has many. Study the movement with a friend and you will not only discover the meaning, you may even create new uses!

366   367   368

K. SNAKE POSTURE (SHE)

The function of this posture is the rearward strike or a two-handed push while turning. It is an excellent one to go into from a variation of the *Single Change*. As you walk with your right palm in the center, toe-in your left foot to your right foot *(Figs. 377–378)*. So far, this conforms to the *Single Change* you have learned. But now, instead of doing a toe-out with your right foot, extending your right arm, and going to it with a left foot toe-in, you simply turn to the rear by thrusting your right palm back under your right armpit *(Fig. 379)*. At the same time, turn your right foot to the new direction *(Fig. 380)*. The *Single Change* can now be made by simply bringing your left foot to toe-in near your right foot and taking your left arm under your right elbow as you stretch to the right as far as you can with both palms turned upward. Then you swing back to the left, gradually carrying your left palm into the

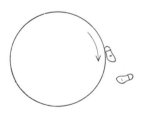

148

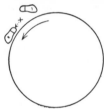

center. This is a speedier *Single Change* than the one you have learned. But the *Snake Posture* eschews the final toe-in. As you thrust backward with your right palm under your armpit, turn your right toes to the right and, turning your left palm upward, extend it as your right hand, palm down, is carried to a point near your forehead *(Figs. 381–382)*. Now you simply walk the circle with the left hand, palm up, in the center *(Fig. 383)*. Kuo liked this method, but often called it *Pai Hao* (Stork). The name is not important, the technique is. So learn it well.

L. LION POSTURE (SZU)

With your right arm in the center, walk the circle *(Fig. 384)*. Make the *Single Change*. At its conclusion, as you swing to the left with your left foot ahead, separate your arms, stretching the left horizontally, palm up, into the center, and carry your right biceps up near your right ear with the right palm up (Figs. 385–387 show the posture from three different vantages). Your "tiger mouths" are aligned diagonally downward, as if you were holding a rod between them. Continue walking in this way. By twisting your palms downward and lowering your right arm you return to the basic walking posture. To change directions, simply make the *Single Change* and reverse the directions above. The use is in the deflecting right hand and the shooting left palm. The first part of Sun's *Phoenix Posture* is similar to the *Lion Posture* except that in the former the right arm, with biceps beside your right ear, has the palm down, simulating holding a large ball *(Fig. 388)*.

150

386

387

388

151

389

M. STANDING PALM POSTURE (LI CHANG)

With your left arm in the center, walk the counterclockwise circle *(Fig. 389)*. Make the *Single Change*. Following this, as you swing to the right with your right foot ahead, separate your arms and twist your elbows down. Your palms are twisted so that the palms are up (as if holding two bowls of water) and are at the level of your mouth, directionally aligned to your shoulders. Your eyes gaze at a point midway between your two hands (Figs. 390–392 show the posture from three different vantages). Let your shoulders droop. Walk a while like this and then make the *Single Change*, swinging back and walking counterclockwise with the *Standing*

152

390 391 392

Palm. After some turns, practice repelling an enemy's rear attack from this posture. Toe-in your right foot near your left foot as your right hand circles above your head and your left circles near your right side *(Figs. 393–394)*. At the same time swing your upper torso leftward. Stand on your right foot and continue circling your right

393 394

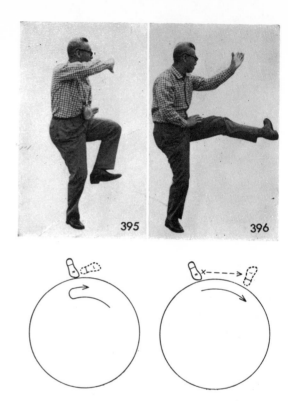

395

396

hand down past your head *(Fig. 395)*. As you thrust out with your left foot, your left palm shoots out over your lowering right arm *(Fig. 396)*. Put your left foot down and continue walking, or make the *Single Change (Figs. 397–398)*. A variant of this is Sun's *White Monkey Offers Fruits*. But in this posture your elbows are almost touching *(Fig. 399)*.

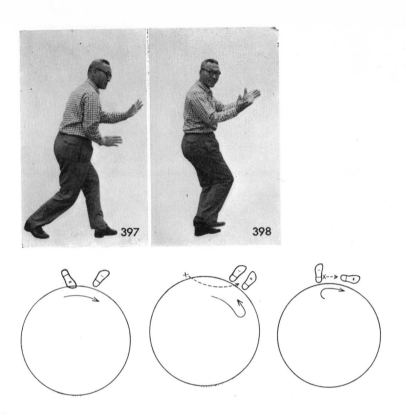

400

401

402

403

156

N. DRAGON POSTURE (LUNG)

With your right arm in the center, walk the circle *(Fig. 400)*. Make the *Single Change*. At its conclusion, as you swing leftward with your left foot ahead, separate your arms, the left to the left, the right to the right, until they form a nearly straight line. Your palms are up as if holding two bowls of water. Your eyes look at your left index finger, which is in the center of the circle. Let your shoulders droop. Contract your inner thighs and hold your head straight as if something were balanced on it *(Fig. 401)*. Your waist accompanies your left hand. To change directions, simply toe-in your right foot and make the *Single Change*, at the conclusion of which you swing rightward. A variant method is called *Two Hands Uphold Flatly (Shuang Chang P'ing T'o)*. In this, the palms are about level with the eyes (Figs. 402–403 show both directions). The same function as that for *Standing Palm Posture* obtains (in Huang's book it is termed *Body Turn with Cutting Leg*).

404

O. HAWK POSTURE (YAO)

With your right palm in the center, walk the circle *(Fig. 404)*.
Begin the *Single Change* by bringing your left foot toed-in beside
your right foot. Then toe-out your right foot and extend your
right arm with the right thumb pointing down. Again toe-in your
left foot near your right foot and, simultaneously, take your left
palm on a diagonal line upward from under your right forearm.
After stretching your left arm as far as you can, turn it clockwise
and thrust it back under your left armpit to the rear *(Fig. 405)*.
At the same time, raise your right foot beside your left knee, and
shoot your right hand, palm up, out from under your chin as your
torso bows slightly *(Fig. 406)*. Next, put your right foot down

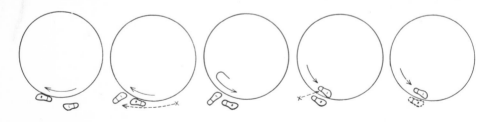

405

406

407

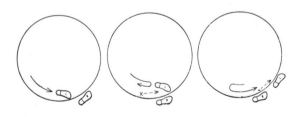

directly ahead and turn your right palm so it is outward, the thumb down, and twist your left hand toward the front. Take your left foot up to toe-in near your right foot as your right palm twists to face up and your left twists under your right elbow until your left palm is up. Then, swing leftward with your left hand gradually pointing into the center. Following the *Hawk Posture*, what you have done is to make a *Single Change* to again walk the circle. This posture is from Sun's book and resembles his *Bear Posture*, the only difference being that in the *Bear Posture* you thrust forward with your left palm on a straight (rather than a rising) line, above (instead of below) the right arm, and your body is more bowed than in the *Hawk Posture (Fig. 407)*. The function of these postures needs no explanation.